THE **MAKING** OF THE **MODERN WORLD**

1945 TO THE PRESENT

Food, Population, and the Environment

BOOKS IN THE SERIES

THE **MAKING** OF THE **MODERN WORLD**

1945 TO THE PRESENT

Food, Population, and the Environment

Valerie Tomaselli

SERIES ADVISOR
Ruud van Dijk

Mason Crest

Mason Crest
450 Parkway Drive, Suite D
Broomall, PA 19008
www.masoncrest.com

Produced and developed by MTM Publishing.
www.mtmpublishing.com

President and Project Coordinator: Valerie Tomaselli
Designer: Sherry Williams, Oxygen Design Group
Copyeditor: Lee Motteler, GeoMap Corp.
Editorial Coordinator: Andrea St. Aubin
Proofreader: Peter Jaskowiak

ISBN: 978-1-4222-3637-6
Series ISBN: 978-1-4222-3634-5
Ebook ISBN: 978-1-4222-8281-6

Library of Congress Cataloging-in-Publication Data

Names: Tomaselli, Valerie, author.
Title: Food, population, and the environment / by Valerie Tomaselli.
Description: Broomall, PA : Mason Crest, 2017. | Series: Making of the modern
    world: 1945 to the present | Includes index.
Identifiers: LCCN 2016020060| ISBN 9781422236376 (hardback) | ISBN
    9781422236345 (series) | ISBN 9781422282816 (ebook)
Subjects: LCSH: Food supply. | Population. | Environmental policy. |
    Sustainable development.
Classification: LCC HD9000.5 .T646 2017 | DDC 338.1/9--dc23
LC record available at https://lccn.loc.gov/2016020060

Printed and bound in the United States of America.

First printing
9 8 7 6 5 4 3 2 1

Contents

KEY ICONS TO LOOK FOR:

Words to understand: These words with their easy-to-understand definitions will increase the reader's understanding of the text while building vocabulary skills.

Sidebars: This boxed material within the main text allows readers to build knowledge, gain insights, explore possibilities, and broaden their perspectives by weaving together additional information to provide realistic and holistic perspectives.

Educational Videos: Readers can view videos by scanning our QR codes, providing them with additional educational content to supplement the text. Examples include news coverage, moments in history, speeches, iconic sports moments and much more!

Text-dependent questions: These questions send the reader back to the text for more careful attention to the evidence presented there.

Research projects: Readers are pointed toward areas of further inquiry connected to each chapter. Suggestions are provided for projects that encourage deeper research and analysis.

Series Introduction

In 1945, at the end of World War II, the world had to start afresh in many ways. The war had affected the entire world, destroying cities, sometimes entire regions, and killing millions. At the end of the war, millions more were displaced or on the move, while hunger, disease, and poverty threatened survivors everywhere the war had been fought.

Politically, the old, European-dominated order had been discredited. Western European democracies had failed to stop Hitler, and in Asia they had been powerless against imperial Japan. The autocratic, militaristic Axis powers had been defeated. But their victory was achieved primarily through the efforts of the Soviet Union—a communist dictatorship—and the United States, which was the only democracy powerful enough to aid Great Britain and the other Allied powers in defeating the Axis onslaught. With the European colonial powers weakened, the populations of their respective empires now demanded their independence.

The war had truly been a global catastrophe. It underlined the extent to which peoples and countries around the world were interconnected and interdependent. However, the search for shared approaches to major, global challenges in the postwar world—symbolized by the founding of the United Nations—was soon overshadowed by the Cold War. The leading powers in this contest, the United States and the Soviet Union, represented mutually exclusive visions for the postwar world. The Soviet Union advocated collectivism, centrally planned economies, and a leading role for the Communist Party. The United States sought to promote liberal democracy, symbolized by free markets and open political systems. Each believed fervently in the promise and justice of its vision for the future. And neither thought it could compromise on what it considered vital interests. Both were concerned about whose influence would dominate Europe, for example, and to whom newly independent nations in the non-Western world would pledge their allegiance. As a result, the postwar world would be far from peaceful.

As the Cold War proceeded, peoples living beyond the Western world and outside the control of the Soviet Union began to find their voices. Driven by decolonization, the developing world, or so-called Third World, took on a new importance. In particular, countries in these areas were potential allies on both sides of the Cold War. As the newly independent peoples established their own identities and built viable states, they resisted the sometimes coercive pull of the Cold War superpowers, while also trying to use them for their own ends. In addition, a new Communist China, established in 1949 and the largest country in the developing world, was deeply entangled within the Cold War contest between communist and capitalist camps. Over the coming decades, however, it would come to act ever more independently from either the United States or the Soviet Union.

During the war, governments had made significant strides in developing new technologies in areas such as aviation, radar, missile technology, and, most ominous, nuclear energy. Scientific and technological breakthroughs achieved in a military context held promise for civilian applications, and thus were poised to contribute to recovery and, ultimately, prosperity. In other fields, it also seemed time for a fresh start. For example, education could be used to "re-educate" members of aggressor nations and further Cold War agendas, but education could also help more people take advantage of, and contribute to, the possibilities of the new age of science and technology.

For several decades after 1945, the Cold War competition seemed to dominate, and indeed define, the postwar world. Driven by ideology, the conflict extended into politics, economics, science and technology, and culture. Geographically, it came to affect virtually the entire world. From our twenty-first-century vantage point, however, it is clear that well before the Cold War's end in the late 1980s, the world had been moving on from the East-West conflict.

Looking back, it appears that, despite divisions—between communist and capitalist camps, or between developed and developing countries—the world after 1945 was growing more and more interconnected. After the Cold War, this increasingly came to be called "globalization." People in many different places faced shared challenges. And as time went on, an awareness of this interconnectedness grew. One response by people in and outside of governments was to seek common approaches, to think and act globally. Another was to protect national, local, or private autonomy, to keep the outside world at bay. Neither usually existed by itself; reality was generally some combination of the two.

Thematically organized, the nine volumes in this series explore how the post–World War II world gradually evolved from the fractured ruins of 1945, through the various crises of the Cold War and the decolonization process, to a world characterized by interconnectedness and interdependence. The accounts in these volumes reinforce each other, and are best studied together. Taking them as a whole will build a broad understanding of the ways in which "globalization" has become the defining feature of the world in the early twenty-first century.

However, the volumes are designed to stand on their own. Tracing the evolution of trade and the global economy, for example, the reader will learn enough about the political context to get a broader understanding of the times. Of course, studying economic developments will likely lead to curiosity about scientific and technological progress, social and cultural change, poverty and education, and more. In other words, studying one volume should lead to interest in the others. In the end, no element of our globalizing world can be fully understood in isolation.

The volumes do not have to be read in a specific order. It is best to be led by one's own interests in deciding where to start. What we recommend is a curious, critical stance throughout the study of the world's history since World War II: to keep asking questions about the causes of events, to keep looking for connections to deepen your understanding of how we have gotten to where we are today. If students achieve this goal with the help of our volumes, we—and they—will have succeeded.

—Ruud van Dijk

A Piper J-3 Cub plane, similar to the one Jim Chenault and other World War II pilots used when they entered the crop-dusting business on their return home.

WORDS TO UNDERSTAND

aerobatic: relating to flying tricks with an airplane.

annihilation: complete destruction.

boom: armlike device used to extend the reach of something.

contaminated: polluted.

eradicate: wipe out; destroy.

pesticides: substances, usually chemicals, used to destroy pests, including herbicides that control unwanted plants and insecticides that control unwanted insects.

1

The Effects of World War II

Jim Chenault, a World War II pilot, defied the odds. He survived thirty-two missions over Germany in a period of just two and a half months—when it was nearly impossible, according to statistics, to survive more than twenty-five.

When the war ended in victory for the Allies and Chenault returned to the United States, he had an itch to keep flying. With a business partner, Don Bair, Chenault bought a military trainer plane, a Piper J-3 Cub, and entered the crop-dusting business. Chenault, Bair, and others like them outfitted their planes with a spray tank, a **boom**, and a pump. With often hair-raising tactics, they sprayed chemical **pesticides** on fields to combat weeds and bugs that destroyed crops. These pilots, and the farmers they worked for, knew such chemicals could be dangerous. However, the full extent of the damage they could cause wouldn't be understood for some time.

Crop dusting, a relatively new field by the end of World War II, benefitted in many ways from the war. Not only were trained military pilots anxious to apply the **aerobatic** skills they learned during the war—close-to-the-ground maneuvering and fast-banking climbs. But during the war itself, new chemicals were developed that could be used as pesticides. And many other wartime innovations would come to serve populations and societies as they tried to recover from the effects of the war.

IN THEIR OWN WORDS

Jim Chenault, World War II Pilot and Crop Duster

You had to be a little careful, because you didn't want to get it some place where you didn't want it, because it could kill trees and shrubbery and damage crops. . . . Everybody that flew kind of had a desire to buzz, get close to the ground and get close to things, and whatnot. It kind of adds to that. [Laughs.] But, really it's just about as dangerous as you want to make it. If you've been in the business for a while, you leave yourself leeway to clear objects, and whatnot.

– From an interview for Wessel's Living History Farm Web site.

World War II and the Chemical Industry

The use of chemicals in agriculture, as well as in food preservation, medicine, and the like, sky-rocketed after World War II. The war effort produced new avenues for research, new scientists to conduct research, and new chemical factories to be used for civilian purposes. Advances in agricultural production were needed to feed hungry populations whose croplands were destroyed by the war. Researchers would soon realize, however, that chemicals and other interventions in the environment could also produce devastating effects.

The use of fertilizer, as well as pesticides, grew during the postwar years, applied liberally to cropland to increase food production. Nitrogen, produced in the form of ammonia, became widely available due to its use in TNT, an explosive manufactured and used during the war. According to Wessel's Living History Farm online, the government was producing 730,000 tons (662,244 metric tons) of ammonia annually, in both the new factories it built for the war and older ones. And more than twice could be produced, if needed.

A worker checking the data settings at one of the Tennessee Valley Authority's nitrate plants, converted to military use during the war.

All this excess capacity was available at the end of the war, and growers took advantage of it. More and more farms began to plant just one or two crops, no longer rotating them on a regular basis. These practices depleted the soil of nutrients quickly. Chemical-based fertilizer was an easy fix. Applying anhydrous ammonia—which is 85 percent nitrogen—to their fields helped enrich the soil. The more fertilizer they used, the better the crops grew. By 1950, chemical factories were churning out 2.6 million tons (2.4 metric tons) per year to meet the growing demand. Unforeseen then was the environmental damage caused by chemical fertilizers—problems that would come to light in the coming decades.

Malaria Control and Insecticides

The war effort also resulted in the development of DDT. It was used as an insecticide to control malaria and typhus, two deadly diseases that affected large numbers of civilians and troops in parts of Europe and the Pacific. Pyrethrum, an insecticide made from the crushed heads of daisies, was in short supply during the war. DDT, a chemical alternative easy to manufacture, helped the Allies, in a way, to win the war.

The U.S. Army also set its sights on developing medicinal cures for malaria to supplement quinine, the standard treatment at the time. This concerted effort resulted in the development and approval of Atabrine and chloroquine. These new drugs, plus DDT, were eventually put to use in a worldwide strategy to **eradicate** malaria. The campaign achieved major victories. According to the July 2007 *National Geographic*, "Malaria was virtually wiped out in much of the Caribbean and South Pacific, from the Balkans, from Taiwan. In Sri Lanka, there were 2.8 million cases of malaria in 1946, and a total of 17 in 1963. In India, malaria deaths plummeted from 800,000 a year to scarcely any." Despite these successes, the money for eradication dried up and malaria resurged, including in India and Sri Lanka.

In addition to funding issues, concerns rose about the environmental risks of DDT. Farmers were using it more and more as a general pesticide. It was cheap and unregulated—so applying more, rather than limited amounts, was easy. Excess amounts of DDT **contaminated** the surrounding land as it leached off fields and polluted nearby streams. While relatively safe for humans, except if it accumulates to high levels, it was shown to be toxic to birds and fish. The benefits of DDT aside, its use became highly suspect. And as seen in the next chapter, its reputation would become so tainted that it was banned by most countries for agricultural use.

Other insecticides, as well as herbicides, were developed during and right after the war. The weed killer known as 2,4-D was arguably more important to American farmers than DDT. It was developed in 1944 and released for public testing in 1945. According to Wessel's Living History Farm Web site, 631,000 pounds (286,217 kg) were sold to American growers in 1946, but in just one year that number grew by more than eight times. In the next six years, the United States Department of Agriculture registered 10,000 new pesticide products. The war helped give birth to a whole new chemical age. In the decades that followed, however, the environmental fallout would be felt.

Nuclear Fallout

Science and technology were used to fight the war in other ways. Most notorious were the two atomic bombs dropped on Japan. The first bomb—dropped on Hiroshima on August 6, 1945—killed some 70,000 immediately, and the second—dropped three days later, on Nagasaki—killed upwards of 40,000 people.

A military poster about fighting malaria-carrying mosquitos during World War II.

Within four months, the number of dead at least doubled. The explosion and heat generated by the first bomb completely destroyed 4.4 square miles (11.4 sq. km) around the epicenter in Hiroshima. The one dropped on Nagasaki leveled 1.8 square miles (4.7 sq. km). The land remained contaminated for decades. And the long-term effects of radiation sickness were felt into the 2000s, as the last of the survivors were still living.

A specialist spraying a sheep with DDT to control ticks and other insects in Benton County, Oregon.

The dawning of the Atomic Age, beginning with the dropping of the bombs on Japan, would become a major feature of the Cold War. As tensions between the United States and the Soviet Union mounted, the threat of nuclear war, and even **annihilation**, became real. The nuclear competition between the two superpowers would lead to all sorts of environmental destruction. Radioactive waste from the Hanford Site, established during the war, was dumped into the Columbia River in Washington State. Lake Karachay, a nuclear disposal site in central Russia used by the Soviets, is now one of the most radioactive sites on the planet. Nuclear tests conducted in Nevada, in the Pacific on Bikini and Enewetak Atolls, and in the Arctic Ocean caused unknown and untold contamination and destruction.

As the decades wore on, the power of the atom would be used in the production of energy. Many would feel that nuclear energy was benign and the answer for many countries without enough access to other forms of energy. But its potential danger concerned people across the world. Not only did the possibility for accidents alarm the public, but the concern about the safe disposal of nuclear waste vexed technologists as well as policy makers. Many wondered whether nuclear power could ever be made completely safe for humanity or the planet we live on.

A nuclear waste storage facility being built at Onkalo, on the west coast of Finland. Spent nuclear fuel will be deposited deep underground, in the granite bedrock, accessed through tunnels such as this.

Text-Dependent Questions

1. Name one of the two main drugs developed during World War II to treat malaria.

2. What is anhydrous ammonia?

3. Name two environmental impacts of World War II.

Research Projects

1. Search for information on the use of DDT in the decades since World War II, and create a line or bar graph showing its increase and decrease. Create a pie graph showing the share of DDT use in each region of the world compared to the total.

2. Prepare a short report on chemical and natural fertilizers, including the reason for their uses, the positive effects, and the negative consequences. Use data and specific examples to support your claims. Present your findings to your class.

ABOVE: A World War II Canadian War Cemetery in Holten, the Netherlands.

WORDS TO UNDERSTAND

benign: without harm.

endemic: native to or belonging to a specific country or region.

fathom: to understand the full meaning of.

humanitarian: relating to human well-being and alleviating suffering.

repatriation: return to home.

scuba: equipment to allow an individual to breathe underwater; typically involving air stored in a tank attached to a person's back.

CHAPTER

2

Growing Populations, Recovering Economics

World War II was the deadliest war in human history. While statistics vary, the estimates run from 50 million to 80 million—the higher number including deaths due to disease and famine. Compared to the world's prewar population, the percentage of dead ranges from 2.1 to 3.4 percent. This devastation was also reflected in economic losses, including in agriculture. Germany, on its own, lost 35 percent of its agricultural production compared to prewar levels.

Loss and Recovery

On a country-by-country basis, casualty figures from World War II are hard to **fathom**. In Europe, Poland lost approximately 17 percent of its prewar population; Germany, around 8 percent; and Hungary, around 7 percent.

The Soviet Union's losses were staggering: 14 percent of the prewar population died during the conflict, but individual republics suffered much higher losses. In Belarus, for instance, 25 percent died, and in the Ukraine, 16 percent. The two small Baltic republics of Latvia and Lithuania suffered losses of approximately 12.5 and 14.3 percent, respectively. Russia itself lost 13 percent of its prewar population.

In Asia, Japan's war-related deaths ranged from 3.5 to 4.5 percent of its prewar population, numbering 2.5 to 3.2 million, and China lost from 2.9 to 3.9 percent—numbering 15 to 20 million. On the other hand, small island nations of the Pacific, where fierce fighting took place, suffered heavy casualties, compared to already small populations. Nauru, an Australian possession, lost only 500 people, but that amounted to over 14 percent of the island's population. In the Philippines, then a U.S. territory, 3.3 percent of its prewar population, or 527,000 people, perished in the war.

After the war, populations in nearly all regions of the world began to recover quickly. Population booms occurred in Europe, in Asia, and in North America. With soldiers returning from the front—joining their wives or soon to marry—natural birthrates skyrocketed. All countries involved in the war also gained population through **repatriation** of soldiers and refugees who fled during the war. This phenomenon was felt more keenly by countries on the front lines, such as Germany, Japan, and Russia. Slowly, lives were getting back to normal.

Baby Boom

A baby boom occurred in almost all countries involved in the war, from the United States to Britain, Germany, and other European countries; from Japan to China and Australia. The exact years vary from country to country—and even within countries, the years are subject to debate—but the number of births in the postwar period did markedly increase.

For most nations, the surge began right after the war, as soldiers returned home. In the United States, France, Britain, Hungary, and Australia, to name a few, the boom started in 1946. Canada's began a year later, as the soldiers took longer to return home than those in the United States. In countries more affected by the war, the baby boom was considerably delayed. In Germany, for instance, it didn't really begin until around 1955. Poland, under the influence of the Soviet Union during the Cold War, experienced a similar lag.

The Soviet Union itself didn't experience a bounce in births at all. In fact, a widespread famine hit the communist country in 1946—with the strongest effects felt in the grain-producing areas of central Russia, Moldova, and the Ukraine. The famine was exacerbated by the economic and demographic devastation of war, including the loss of able-bodied men and the lack of equipment to work the fields.

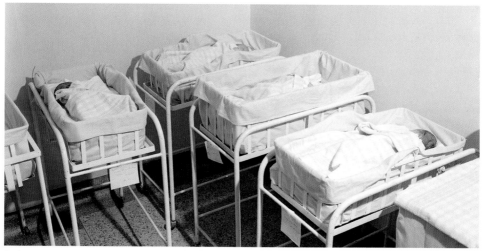

Babies in a nursery in Virginia, in 1946; a boom in births occurred in nearly all countries that fought in the war.

The production of a new car at the Fiat plant in Italy, made possible by funds from the Marshall Plan.

Economic Rebound

The rise in births occurred hand in hand with economic recovery. Building tanks, airplanes, and bombs put more people to work in the United States, in effect ending the Great Depression, which had preceded World War II. Feeding large armies required agricultural land to be plowed again. In the United States, at least, few areas of economic activity were not called into service during the war.

After the war, pent-up demand, along with economic support from governments, completed the transformation. In the United States, the GI Bill helped soldiers returning from the war acquire an education, encouraged them to buy homes, and helped them begin families. On a global scale, the U.S.-funded Marshall Plan helped entire countries boost their economies. In an effort to shore up allies in the Cold War, the plan funded projects that helped war-torn countries expand industrial production, mechanize agriculture, and develop infrastructure. The Soviet Union, meanwhile, brought Eastern Europe under its influence behind what Britain's Winston Churchill famously dubbed "an Iron Curtain."

As economies improved in Western countries, a growing middle class emerged. Consumerism—the reliance on material goods to live a good life—fueled the recovery. Families in the 1950s in the United States and Europe bought televisions and washing machines, and they purchased refrigerators and freezers, as well as food to fill them with.

Feeding Growing Populations

Countries of the Third World were also experiencing earthshaking changes. Following the war, decolonization took center stage. European colonial powers, weakened by the war, soon lost or gave up their colonial possessions. The newly created United Nations even wrote the principles of equal rights and self-government of independent peoples into its charter. As countries in Africa and Asia took up the mantle of self-determination, they also faced the challenges of feeding their growing populations. Famine and low agricultural output were **endemic** in many parts of these areas.

Science, however, provided an answer in the form of a "Green Revolution." It began in Mexico a decade after the war, through the research of Dr. Norman Borlaug, a plant pathologist, and under a joint Mexico–Rockefeller Foundation development program. Borlaug's work focused on developing new strains of plants, including wheat, that were disease resistant and could withstand harsh climates.

In hopes of increasing crop yields and boosting food security, Borlaug created a dwarf strain of wheat. A shorter stem would help the plant stay upright throughout the growing season. His success in Mexico—increasing the wheat-crop yield threefold—spread. It led the Indian and Pakistani governments, with help from the Rockefeller Foundation and the UN's Food and Agriculture Organization, to ask him for help in the mid-1960s. This region was facing fast-growing populations as well as famines that had recurred since the 1940s. Borlaug's innovations were applied to rice and wheat in the Indian subcontinent, helping those countries become self-sufficient in food production. They are also credited with saving the lives of perhaps a billion people across the developing world.

Criticism arose around the Green Revolution, however, with many concerned that the new varieties of grains needed large amounts of chemical fertilizer and pesticides to generate high yields. Borlaug and other advocates of the Green Revolution countered those fears by raising **humanitarian** concerns. These practices were necessary, according to them, in the face of skyrocketing population growth and the struggles of developing countries to improve agricultural output.

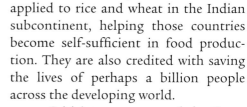

Dr. Norman Borlaug, the plant scientist whose research launched the "Green Revolution."

Sounding an Alarm, Raising Awareness

As science and technology took center stage in food production during the 1950s, more people became concerned. They saw interventions into agriculture and the environment as a risky enterprise. Would pesticides, fertilizer, and other chemicals, for instance, lead to unforeseen, unknowable, and damaging effects on the environment?

Rachel Carson is credited with first bringing these issues to a wide audience. Carson was trained both as a writer and marine biologist. She worked from 1940 to 1952 at the U.S. Fish and Wildlife Service, where she was in charge of their publications program. While there, she published her first book, *Under the Sea Wind* (1941), which introduced readers to her brand of nature writing, as she portrayed the wonder and complexity of the marine environment. Her second book, *The Sea Around Us* (1951), was her first best seller, earning her a National Book Award.

Silent Spring, published in 1962, secured her legacy in the modern environmental movement. In the book, she warned about pesticides in food production and the long-term effects of chemicals on the environment and on human health. Her warnings were specific and backed up with documentation. DDT, for example, was a particular concern for Carson, especially while working at the National Audubon Society. In *Silent Spring*, she presented evidence of DDT's effect on bird populations and noted that DDT was classified as a carcinogen, associated with liver cancer in mice in the laboratory tests.

Carson was denounced by the chemical industry for "gross distortion of the actual facts." But her criticism stuck and she held firm. In testimony before the U.S. Congress in

GENETIC MODIFICATION, THEN AND NOW

Borlaug's work was a major factor in the development of modern plant-breeding techniques. Creating new strains of plants by cross-breeding them with different varieties to develop desirable traits over generations was a benign precursor, in a way, to genetic engineering.

Producing genetically modified organisms (GMOs) involves manipulating genetic material at the cellular level. In the last two decades of the twentieth century, developing GMOs was one of the most active innovations in agriculture. The first U.S. patent for a GMO was issued in 1980, and the first GMO food—a slow-ripening tomato—hit U.S. grocery shelves in 1994. By 1997, the European Union was requiring foods made with GMO ingredients to be labeled as such. By the 2010s, GMOs dominated food production across the globe. At the same time, critics of a GMO-based food supply have grown more and more vocal.

Rachel Carson (on right), author of *Silent Spring*, which helped to launch the modern environmental movement; she is pictured here with Robert Hines, a staff illustrator with the U.S. Fish and Wildlife Service, on the Atlantic Coast. Hines illustrated Carson's *Under the Sea Wind*.

A CASE FOR DDT?

The campaign against malaria, launched in 1955 under the direction of the World Health Organization, truly saved lives. The combined use of DDT and chloroquine reduced the incidence of the disease worldwide. And by 1961, ironically one year before *Silent Spring* was published, the worldwide antimalaria campaign had eradicated the disease in thirty-seven countries. But its efficacy was challenged when some strains of the mosquitoes responsible for spreading the disease developed resistance to DDT.

In 2001, DDT was banned internationally for agricultural use, under the Stockholm Convention on Persistent Organic Pollutants. The convention, however, still allowed DDT to be used to control malaria. And in 2006, the World Health Organization again stood behind it, recommending DDT to fight malaria in countries where the disease hits the hardest. Despite this official approval, its use is still controversial. Many argue that controlling malaria is possible through other means, such as the systematic use of bed netting or screens and draining standing water where mosquitoes breed.

1963, she urged the government to adopt policies that would protect humans and the environment from the harmful effects of toxins in the environments. U.S. president John F. Kennedy's Science Advisory Committee confirmed the validity of Carson's claims. By 1971, the use of DDT was banned in the United States.

During the same time period, across the Atlantic, a French naval officer and undersea explorer was raising awareness of the complex world under the ocean's surface. Jacques Cousteau, credited with inventing the aqualung, a precursor to today's **scuba** gear, published *The Silent World: A Story of Undersea Discovery and Adventure* in 1953. Three years later he turned the book into a documentary film, one that caught the attention of viewers in Europe and North America.

While criticized in some circles for the damage the crew did to the seabed during filming, the movie introduced readers to the beauty of undersea life. The film was one of the first to use underwater color film. And just as color television was spreading, his series, *The Undersea World of Jacques Cousteau*, was broadcast in Britain and the United States. Cousteau would later become a strong advocate for environmental stewardship and became involved in marine conservation.

Jacques Cousteau's *Denise*, a "diving saucer," the world's first submersible "vehicle" designed for underwater exploration, being raised to the surface.

Text-Dependent Questions

1. What country discussed in this chapter did not experience a post–World War II baby boom?

2. Who was Norman Borlaug, and what was the Green Revolution?

3. Which book by Rachel Carson was important in launching the modern environmental movement?

Research Projects

1. Research one of the individuals mentioned in this chapter. Write a brief biography of at least four paragraphs, focusing on their education, work, and environmental legacy.

2. Prepare for a debate on the use of DDT for controlling malaria. Begin with the information in this chapter, but find data, information, and analysis from respected sources, such as the World Health Organization and the Centers for Disease Control, in your library or online. Prepare an opening statement taking a pro or con stance.

Educational Video

Jacques-Yves Cousteau
Page 20
A video biography of the world-famous French undersea explorer.

Published on YouTube by Rocketboom.
https://youtu.be/KdSipdXBStA.

WORDS TO UNDERSTAND

drought: period of extreme dryness and lack of rainfall.

dysfunctional: managed, operating, or functioning poorly.

geopolitical: relating to power based on political and territorial control.

sectors: divisions or parts, here especially of an economy.

sterilization: procedure to remove the reproductive abilities of an individual.

think tank: group—often of academics and policy makers—dedicated to analyzing and solving problems.

ABOVE: Population growth became a growing concern in the 1960s and 1970s. And while growth rates have not hit the highs expected at that time, they are still very high in many developing countries. Pictured here is an overcrowded neighborhood in Delhi, India.

CHAPTER

3

Population Explosion?

In the 1960s, as concern was mounting about environmental degradation, population growth seemed to be a potential time bomb. With the Earth's capacity to produce enough food at a limited level, the prospects for survival, especially in poorer regions of the world, were called into question. This, along with pollution, deforestation, and other environmental issues, increased the anxiety of many already troubled by the threats posed by the Cold War and the Atomic Age.

Sounding an Alarm

Paul Ehrlich's *The Population Bomb* was published in 1968, sounding a huge alarm about the pressure that population growth was putting on the world's resources. Co-written with his wife, Anne Ehrlich (who didn't receive credit as an author), the book claimed that an ongoing "population explosion" would result in hunger and starvation for masses of people. Ehrlich pointed to the fact that the world's population doubled from 1930 to the mid-1960s. He projected that it would double again in another thirty or so years.

The book urged immediate action to curtail population growth. Many of his suggestions targeted the United States, given the size of its population and the huge amount of the Earth's resources the country consumed. They included such measures as higher taxes for families who had more children. **Sterilization** of men was also proposed. Recommendations for other countries sound equally extreme to today's observers. For instance, it was recommended that international food aid should be cut off for those countries, such as India, whose food security problems, due to huge population growth, were deemed impossible to fix.

The Population Bomb became a best seller and raised awareness of the effect of humanity on the Earth's resources. Many of the specific predictions made in the book, however, did not come to pass. One was the claim that the planet's population would double from the mid-1960s to the mid-1990s. Also, Ehrlich forecasted a huge increase in the death rate in the 1970s due to massive famines that would threaten

THE LIMITS TO GROWTH

Paul Ehrlich, author of *The Population Bomb,* pictured here in 2010.

In 1972 another book—*The Limits to Growth*—was published addressing similar issues. The work, authored by Donella H. Meadows, Dennis L. Meadows, and others, was commissioned by the Club of Rome, an international **think tank** comprising heads of state, UN officials, diplomats, economists, business leaders, and scientists. The authors, while at the Massachusetts Institute of Technology, developed a model to project the long-term prospects for the environment and humanity, given the expected trajectory of growth in economic activity, population, and resource use, especially oil.

While the authors insisted that their intention was not to make exact predictions, only to suggest possible trends, two of the scenarios predicted the collapse of economic and population growth by the middle to late twenty-first century. Some criticized the conclusions as alarmist. However, many reviews since the initial report—it has been updated on a regular basis—conclude that most of the important projections match new realities.

food security. The death rate, as measured by the UN and other agencies, has in fact declined since Ehrlich's book was published.

The Facts about Population Growth

Even though Ehrlich's most dire predictions did not pan out, population growth had been rising steeply since the end of World War II. In 1950, the planet was home to 2.5 billion people, according to the UN's *World Population Prospects: 2015 Revision* (UNPP2015); by 1980, it had risen to 4.4 billion. This translates to a 78 percent increase.

This extreme rise reflected several historical trends. As discussed in the previous chapter, all countries involved in the war suffered losses due to fighting, disease, and hunger. A natural increase after hostilities ended was inevitable. Also, the world economy, especially in countries of the Western world, rebounded, and this prosperity translated to more births, resulting in baby booms.

The growth in population in developing countries was also a factor. In 1950, population in "more developed countries," according to the UNPP2015, was 813 million, and in 1980, it was 1,081 million, an increase of 33 percent. In "less developed countries," the population was 1,712 million in 1950 and 3,358 million in 1980—a 96 percent increase. This gap in the growth rate would continue to widen, reflecting general welfare trends in the developing world. More people had access to health care—increasing birthrates and lowering mortality rates—in many developing countries.

India and China were the two most populous countries in the world in 1950—and they still are today. Both countries have faced serious challenges in feeding their growing nations. During the years 1959 to 1961, for instance, China suffered a devastating famine. According to varying estimates, 15 to 43 million people died as a result of the famine. It took place during the Great Leap Forward, a modernization program under Chairman Mao Zedong that called for a drastic reorganization of agriculture and economic life—all geared toward the country's rapid industrialization. Under one policy, farming communities and urban neighborhoods were required to start backyard steel furnaces to help increase steel output. Agricultural production dropped drastically, as peasants went so far as to melt their farm equipment in the furnaces.

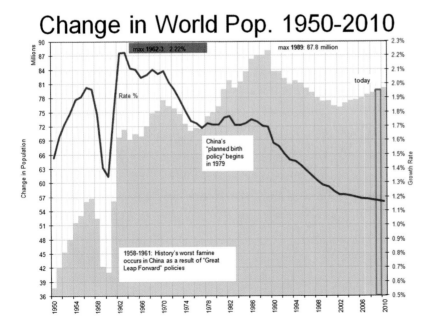

Change in World Pop. 1950-2010

max 1962.3 2.22%

max 1989 87.8 million

today

Rate %

China's "planned birth policy" begins in 1979

1958-1961: History's worst famine occurs in China as a result of "Great Leap Forward" policies

This chart shows the yearly change in population from 1950 to 2010. The red line marks the growth rate, and the bars in grey mark the actual increase in numbers of people every year. Also noted are key events in China's population trends, including the massive famine in 1959-1961.

The government blamed the famine on natural disasters and **drought**. Many historians, however, say that weather trends only played a small part in the disaster. Still, China's Communist Party called it "Three Years of Natural Disasters," while many peasants referred to the period as "Three Bitter Years."

Feeding the Developing World

The population of the developing world, as noted earlier, had grown at the highest rates of any other part of the world. With greater access to health care and birth control, birthrates were high. And those live births were important to families struggling to survive. Many of the world's least-developed countries were still dependent on farming for their own food and livelihood. The more children a family had, the more help they had to work the fields and tend to household chores.

But increases in population were still outpacing increases in food production. Efforts to produce heartier plants and increase crop yields, such as those of the Green Revolution (discussed in the previous chapter), helped to alleviate massive famine and deaths due to hunger and lack of nourishment. But they, too, came with a price—as the plant varieties needed greater and greater amounts of pesticides and fertilizers to achieve maximum yields.

Many poorer countries were newly independent and struggling to establish effective governments. They were plagued by **dysfunctional** management, underfunded budgets, and weak private **sectors**. They didn't yet have the capacity to implement policies and programs to help improve farming or increase emergency food assistance during famines.

International Aid and the Cold War

Both sides of the Cold War divide began to address food security and hunger during the late 1950s and early 1960s, sometimes as a direct tool of **geopolitical** competition. This help was designed to assist poorer countries in modernizing their economies. Both the United States and the Soviet Union angled their assistance toward expanding their influence. This was especially fruitful, as formal colonies gained independence from their European masters and their allegiance was not yet solidified.

An official U.S. postal stamp—in the amount of five cents—issued in 1963 celebrating the Food for Peace program, established under U.S. president Harry S. Truman.

USAID has been active in crisis zones, responding to emergencies, since its founding in 1961. Here, bulgur, a form of wheat, is being unloaded in Haiti in 2010, following a massive earthquake there.

In the United States, President Harry S. Truman's 1950 Point Four Program aimed to improve economic prospects in the developing world in order to create new markets for the United States. One goal was also to attract developing countries to the capitalist system, steering them away from communism. The Office of Food for Peace was signed into law in 1954 under President Dwight D. Eisenhower for similar purposes.

International aid flourished after USAID was launched in 1961 under President John F. Kennedy. Food aid became more responsive to countries in need, separate from the interests of American farmers. Other Western countries later joined in. Australia, for instance, established the Australian Development Assistance Agency (ADAA) in 1974. Now under AusAID, it was launched to help countries reduce poverty, while advancing Australia's goals and interests.

The Soviets, for their part, also moved on the aid front, although it was considerably limited in the early postwar years while the nation was recovering from the war. During the 1950s, the Soviet Union delivered humanitarian aid during crises, such as famines in India. In Cuba, following the communist revolution there in 1959, the Soviets sustained agriculture on the island by paying high amounts for sugarcane, Cuba's main crop.

Intergovernmental organizations also stepped in to help poorer countries feed their populations. The United Nations, at its inception in 1945, established the Food and Agriculture Organization (FAO) to support countries in improving agriculture, enhancing food security, and improving food safety and nutrition. In 1963 it established the World Food Programme to offer direct food assistance to countries in times of stress and crisis.

By the 1960s, many nongovernmental organizations (NGOs) had become active in humanitarian crises and development efforts. Concern Worldwide launched in 1968 in response to an extreme famine in the Nigerian province of Biafra, for instance, and Save the Children, an NGO dating back to the 1920s, had expansive operations in twenty-six countries by that time. Such international NGOs became indispensable players in the humanitarian and development arena. They raised their own funds, received government subsidies, and became important partners in increasing development aid.

The International Committee of the Red Cross delivering food relief during the famine in Biafra in 1968.

Text-Dependent Questions

1. What was one proposal Paul Ehrlich made to curb population growth in *The Population Bomb*?

2. What was the Point Four Program?

3. What was the Great Leap Forward?

Research Projects

1. Research the history of the World Food Programme (WFP) and select one food security emergency it helped to address in the last decade. Prepare a class presentation, being sure to include information on the cause of the crisis, its scope in terms of area, numbers of people it affected, and what the WFP did to address it.

2. Find a copy of the original 1968 edition of *The Population Bomb* online or at your library; one is available at Project Avalon (http://projectavalon.net/The_Population_Bomb_Paul_Ehrlich.pdf). Break off into groups to study the cover of the book and analyze each element: how the title is printed, the text describing the book, and any images on it. Discuss each part—including its factual meaning and the emotional content behind it.

The results of deforestation in the Amazon Rain Forest.

WORDS TO UNDERSTAND

biodiversity: condition of having a wide variety in types of living things, usually measured in the number of different species.

meltdowns: dangerous overheating episodes of a nuclear reactor's core.

mitigation: process of reducing the bad impact of something.

refrigerants: substances that are used to cool an environment.

signatories: individuals, companies, or countries that sign an agreement to abide by a set of rules.

smog: foglike condition in the air resulting from pollution.

Environmental Concerns Increase, Environmentalism Advances

In the 1970s and 1980s, several events across the world increased alarm on the environmental front. Chemical contamination of rivers and lakes, air pollution from power plants and manufacturing facilities, out-of-control extraction of minerals for industrial and military use, nuclear **meltdowns**—all these and more contributed to mounting worldwide anxiety about what humanity was doing to the planet.

Individuals, countries, and international groups began to take action. Western nations saw the first buds of environmental activism coalesce around protecting the Earth. And as Eastern Bloc countries experienced the same kinds of ecological destruction, they too took part, as did the developing world, often reaching over geopolitical divides to take action.

Deforestation

Deforestation in the Amazon and other rain forests became a clarion call for many native peoples and environmental activists in the 1970s and 1980s. In 1988, the murder of Chico Mendes was widely reported outside of his native Brazil. Mendes was a rubber harvester who unionized his fellow tappers to help protect the Amazon from ranchers and developers. At their urging, the government set aside preserves of rubber trees, which protected the rain forest along with the rubber harvesters' livelihoods. The death of Mendes—at the hands of a rancher who tried to expand his holdings and log one of the preserves—followed that of two other rubber organizers, Vincente Cañas in 1987 and Wilson Pinheiro in 1980.

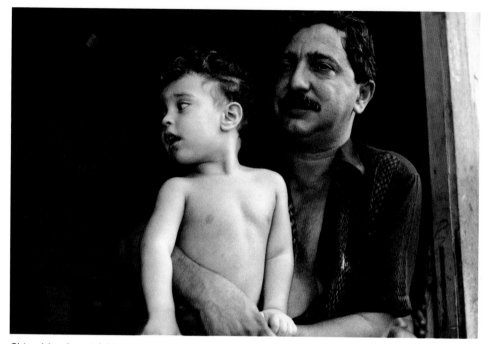

Chico Mendes with his son Sandino, in a photo taken five weeks before Chico was killed.

Other native peoples around the world worked aggressively to save their forests, which were integral to their cultures and ways of life. In 1988, for instance, the Penan people of Sarawak, reliant on the rain forests of Borneo, began organizing to stop timbering there. Like other indigenous hunter-gatherer groups remaining in the world, the survival of their land is critical to their survival.

As activists lost their lives and grassroots groups organized, incremental success was achieved. In 1989, for instance, Brazil, Bolivia, Columbia, Ecuador, Suriname, Peru, Guyana, and Venezuela signed the Amazon Declaration. This accord advocated for the preservation of "our Amazon heritage" and promoted "the rational use of the resources of the region, so that present and future generations may benefit from this legacy of nature."

Air and Water Pollution

Public concern about pollution grew in industrialized nations in the middle of the twentieth century, when disasters made news. In 1952, high levels of **smog** hit London, causing the immediate death of some 4,000 people. Thousands more died in the following weeks. The incident led to Britain's 1956 Clean Air Act, one of the earliest attempts in the modern era to reduce the effects of air pollution.

The disastrous effects of water pollution were seen in 1952 when the Cuyahoga

River in Ohio caught fire. In a highly industrialized area, the river had been considered one of the most polluted in the United States. It had been the scene of many fires created by oil discharged from factories. While the fire in 1952 was the worst in its history—causing over 1 million dollars in damages—another in 1969 eventually helped lead to the Clean Water Act when it drew attention from *Time* magazine. The 1972 law was revised and updated in 1977 and again, with the Water Quality Act, in 1987.

It was during the 1970s that U.S. federal government began to address environmental concerns at the national level, no longer leaving them to local and state authorities. The National Environmental Policy Act, in 1970, established the country's Environmental Protection Agency. The Clean Air Act was passed in 1970, and the Safe Drinking Water Act, which addressed groundwater pollution, was passed in 1974.

Air and water pollution were also growing concerns in newly industrializing countries. For instance, in Asia, sulfur dioxide emissions had risen dramatically during the 1980–1996 period, due primarily to India and China's reliance on coal for the generation of electricity. India passed air pollution legislation in 1981 and amended it in 1987 to address this issue.

THE BERN CONVENTION, 1963

One of the first international agreements to fight pollution was hammered out by France, Germany, Luxembourg, the Netherlands, and Switzerland. In 1963 these five countries joined forces to help rehabilitate the Rhine, a river flowing through all these countries, and one of the most active industrial waterways in Europe. Their goals were to investigate and monitor the pollution in the river, to begin to restore its health, and to protect against future contamination. Later agreements, with the full support of the European Union, would update and replace many of the accord's provisions.

The Oceans and Marine Environments

Concern about water pollution is truly global when it comes to the oceans. The Mediterranean Sea is a good example. While tiny compared to the entire area that the world's oceans occupy, the Mediterranean is one of the most "international" of waters. According to Greenpeace International's Web site, "nineteen nations border it, more than 10,000 species live in it,

The 1952 fire on the Cuyahoga River in an industrialized region of Ohio, resulting from oil being released from factories along the river.

and millions of people get food, work and pleasure from it." In 1976, sixteen nations adopted the Mediterranean Action Plan (MAP) to address concerns with pollution in the waters. It was revised in 1987 to adapt to what the countries had learned in the first phase.

But according to the United Nations Environment Programme's *Mediterranean Action Plan–1976 to 2006* report, "millions of tons of pollutants" were still being dumped into the waters of the Mediterranean annually. Most of the pollution comes from industries such as metal and chemical factories, oil refineries, tanneries, and food processing plants, to name only a few.

While tightening national and regional regulations is critical, global standards for global resources such as the oceans are critical. In 1982, a prime example, the UN Convention on the Law of the Sea (UNCLOS), was adopted by the United Nations. It entered into force in 1994, and as of 2015, 166 countries, as well as the European Union, have signed on to it. The United States has not, however, a failure that severely limits the impact of UNCLOS. Another weakness in this, as well as other such international agreements, is implementation. The convention's standing in international law is uncertain, so the mechanisms for enforcement are unclear.

Accumulated trash and waste washed up on a beach in Thailand.

Going Nuclear

Another growing cause for concern was nuclear energy. By the early 1950s, during the first decade of the Cold War, Britain, Canada, and the United States had invested heavily in nuclear energy. While France's program developed a bit later—its first nuclear power plant came on line in 1962—it would become the most reliant on nuclear power of any of the Western countries.

In a geopolitical twist, U.S. president Dwight D. Eisenhower launched the Atoms for Peace program in 1953. In a speech before the United Nations, Eisenhower proclaimed that nuclear technology should be used for peaceful purposes—not just for energy, but for advances in medicine and other peaceful ends. He also called for controlling the destructive power of nuclear technology—one of the first demands for limiting the nuclear arms race between the United States and the Soviet Union. His speech helped lead to the creation, in 1956, of the International Atomic Energy Agency (IAEA). The IAEA became the main international organization to control the spread of nuclear weapons.

Another source of energy—oil—took center stage in geopolitics in the 1970s. The Organization of the Petroleum Exporting Countries (OPEC)—founded in 1960 and composed mostly of Arab countries in the Middle East—controlled most of the world's oil production. From its founding, OPEC sought to increase member states' share in oil profits, at the expense of Western-based interests: multinational companies, prior to OPEC, had owned much of the petroleum infrastructure in oil-rich countries.

In 1973, OPEC greatly reduced the amount of oil on international markets, in response to the Yom Kippur War between Israel and its Arab neighbors. As a result, inexpensive oil from OPEC countries could no longer be counted on. Nuclear power came to be viewed as a viable alternative for many countries without oil reserves of their own. France ramped up its nuclear program the year after the crisis, for instance. And Brazil began its production of ethanol, a by-product of corn and other crop production, as a component of gasoline in 1975.

Oregon, like many states in the United Sates, dropped the highway speed limit to 50 mph during the oil crisis of 1973, as a way of addressing gas shortages resulting from the cutback in oil output from OPEC countries.

Nuclear Problems

A series of accidents, however, would seriously taint the reputation of nuclear energy. Early on, Canada experienced one of the first major nuclear energy accidents. In 1952, its reactor at Chalk River in the province of Ontario suffered a partial meltdown. In the United States, the first major event occurred in 1979 at the Three Mile Island Nuclear Generating Station in Pennsylvania. A partial meltdown occurred after the leak of a large amount of coolant used to control the temperature of the reactor's core. This released radioactive material into the environment. The accident resulted from multiple failures, including human errors and mechanical issues. The complexity of the circumstances led many to believe that nuclear reactors were too complicated to ever be made fail-safe. While serious, long-term health consequences were more limited than initially thought, the accident provoked a public outcry and calls by activists to limit nuclear energy.

In 1986 the most serious nuclear accident of all time occurred in the Ukraine, then part of the Soviet Union, at the Chernobyl Nuclear Power Plant in the town of Pripyat. A series of explosions, followed by a fire, destroyed the reactor, its containment vessel, and the building housing it. The accident released massive amounts of radioactive material. The contaminated air spread across much of the western Soviet Union and Europe. The death toll reached thirty-one people, but the long-term health effects from the toxins released into the air, as well as the enduring contamination of the soil, water, and even buildings surrounding the site, are still being felt.

An abandoned house in the "dead zone" around Pripyat, in the Ukraine, after the nuclear accident there in 1986.

Fossil Fuels

Nuclear power was being developed as one of the alternatives to the fossil-fuel-based energy that modern life had come to rely on. Petroleum, coal, and natural gas—the main types of fossil fuels used for energy production—had long been extracted from the Earth and converted to usable forms of energy. Coal, in particular, helped to fuel the Industrial Revolution, which began in the mid-1700s, and petroleum came into use in the mid-to-late 1800s. But, as was being discovered in the late 1900s, the use of fossil fuels was problematic for the environment.

Oil spills occurred with increasing frequency, starting in the late 1970s. Some of the first spills from oil tankers included those off the coast of northern France in 1978 and Trinidad and Tobago in the Caribbean Sea in 1979. Perhaps the best-known early spill in this period was from the *Exxon Valdez*, which ran aground in 1989 off the coast of Alaska. While relatively small in volume compared to others, its environmental impact was initially huge due to the rich **biodiversity** of the region. The area is also remote, so getting help to the area was very difficult.

Emissions from fossil fuels also added to people's anxieties. The idea of climate change was not new in 1988 when the UN's International Panel on Climate Change (IPCC)—now considered the international authority on the science behind climate change—was set up. In 1958 the American scientist Charles Keeling began observing rising seasonal carbon dioxide (CO_2) levels in the atmosphere at the Mauna Loa Observatory in Hawaii. By 1961 he concluded that CO_2 levels were rising on a yearly basis. His measurements resulted in the Keeling Curve, which shows CO_2 rising across decades, and it is considered by many to be a powerful piece of evidence linking carbon dioxide and global warming.

A TWENTY-FIRST CENTURY DISASTER

The *Exxon Valdez* spill, considered one of the worst ecological disasters during the early environmental movement, was eclipsed two decades later by the explosion on the *Deepwater Horizon*, an oil drilling rig owned by BP Petroleum, and the spill that resulted. In 2010, the accident killed eleven crew members and discharged 172-180 million gallons (651-681 million liters) of crude oil into the Gulf of Mexico. The spill devastated seafood populations and marine life in the Gulf Coast, an area just recovering from the ravages of Hurricane Katrina in 2005.

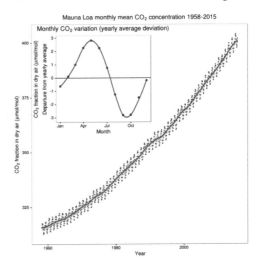

The Keeling curve, based on measurements taken at the Mauna Loa Observatory in Hawaii, starting in 1961 by Charles Keeling. The inset shows the seasonal changes in carbon levels.

The science of global warming, based on the greenhouse effect, is fairly easy to understand. Much like an actual greenhouse where plants are raised, the greenhouse effect naturally helps to warm the surface of the Earth. Carbon dioxide, methane, nitrous oxide, and water vapor—all greenhouse gases—radiate energy in the form of heat to the Earth's surface, keeping it warm enough to support life.

However, as the modern era advanced and the use of fossil fuels increased, greenhouse gases in the atmosphere increased. Automobile engines, factory equipment, home heating systems, and more all generate carbon dioxide and other greenhouse gases. Innumerable aspects of contemporary life—transportation, building, furnaces, household conveniences—can increase, in some way, the amount of greenhouse gasses in the atmosphere. Even deforestation, discussed earlier, which reduces the number of trees that take in carbon dioxide, has played a role. It is responsible for 12 to 17 percent of the annual increase in greenhouse gas emissions, according to the World Resources Institute.

The change in climate—reflected in rising land and ocean temperatures, the melting of polar ice caps, and other indicators—has been analyzed and documented aggressively since the 1980s, when the issue came to the foreground. The fourth assessment of the IPCC, from 2007, noted that from 1995 to that year was the warmest period on record since 1850. It also established that the average annual volume of Arctic sea ice had dropped by 2.7 percent in each of the thirty years since 1978. Increases in the frequency of droughts in Asia and Africa were also documented. And, critically, the IPCC also correlated these changes to a rise in global greenhouse gas emissions that can be traced to human activities. Between 1970 to 2004, that increase was 70 percent. Some observations in recent years, however, have noted what has been termed a "pause" in global temperature rise.

Addressing Climate Change

The worldwide response to climate change has been uneven and slow in coming. In many important ways, the United Nations took the lead. The UN's early efforts to confront environmental issues started in 1972, when it held the Conference on the Human Environment in Stockholm, Sweden. The conference resulted in the establishment of the UN Environment Programme that year, as well as the adoption of the Stockholm Declaration, which outlined twenty-six principles, such as the protection of natural resources and the importance of economic and social development to improving the environment. These goals helped to guide the UN and the international community in their efforts to shape the conversation about the environmental impacts of climate change.

Much scientific and policy activity took place in the 1980s and early 1990s. In 1987 the World Commission on Environment and Development met and issued a report, *Our Common Future*. Also known as the "Brundtland Report," after Norway's prime minister who led the commission, it introduced "sustainable development" into the environmental discussion. It also set the stage for what was to follow, through an action plan called Agenda 21.

At about the same time, in 1988, the UN Environment Programme, along with the UN's World Meteorological Organization, established the IPCC to compile and evaluate scientific research on climate change. The IPCC has issued five assessment reports all together. The first assessment report, in 1990, concluded that human activities were contributing to increased concentrations of greenhouse gases in the atmosphere, which were, in turn, helping to increase global warming. Successive reports, up to the fifth in 2013, would state more clearly the link between human activities and climate change.

The next major international step was the Rio Earth Summit in 1992, which aimed to translate Agenda 21 into action, including an international agreement on climate change. This came in the form of the UN Framework Convention on Climate Change (UNFCCC). The UNFCCC, however, left specifics, such as target emission levels, to a later date, which made it difficult to arrive at an effective agreement. A breakthrough came in 1996 when 150 countries agreed to the Kyoto Protocol, which bound all of the **signatories**, including the United States, to reduce greenhouse emissions. After U.S. president George W. Bush was elected in 2000, however, he withdrew

The melting of sea ice in the polar regions—both north and south—is one of the most serious effects of climate change being tracked by scientists; it's estimated that the extent of sea ice has decreased by 12 percent every decade since the 1970s.

THE OZONE HOLE

In 1985, British researchers discovered an "ozone hole" in the Earth's atmosphere above Antarctica. A layer of ozone surrounds the Earth and filters out parts of the Sun's ultraviolet radiation, which causes sunburn. At high levels it can cause skin cancer, cataracts, and other serious conditions. The researchers found that the deterioration of ozone over the South Pole happened annually, in the spring, as the warmth of the sun warmed the cold atmosphere of the darkened winter months.

Researchers had previously determined that substances called chlorofluorocarbons (CFCs) had a role to play. CFCs are highly stable compounds found in aerosol cans and **refrigerants**. They were responsible for destroying ozone—which on its own is highly unstable. By 1987, under the Montreal Protocol, signed eventually by all members of the United Nations, CFCs were regulated and eventually banned. The ozone layer has recovered as new chemicals were found to perform the same function as CFCs. The type of international agreement that led to the banning of CFCs, however, has not been easy to replicate in the realm of fossil fuel regulation and climate change.

the United States from the protocol, rendering it ineffective. Without the United States, then the largest emitter of greenhouse gases, on board, the worldwide targets would never be met.

The Movement Takes Shape

The increasing public awareness of climate change and other environmental issues went hand in hand with official government and intergovernmental responses. This was also reflected in a growing number of grassroots organizations, as well as domestic political parties that embraced a "green" agenda.

On April 22,1970, environmentalists organized the first Earth Day. Designed as a national "teach-in" and demonstration in support of "planet Earth," it involved up to 20 million people, according to some estimates, across the United States. By 1990, Earth Day had gone global, with some 200 million in 141 countries involved in the day's activities.

Nongovernmental organizations also joined the cause. The World Wildlife Fund (now the World Wide Fund for Nature) was established in 1961, dedicated to protecting and promoting biodiversity on the planet. In 1969, Friends of the Earth split off from the more conservative Sierra Club, one of the oldest environmental groups, founded in 1892 by John Muir, one of the godfathers of the modern environmental movement. Greenpeace was formed in 1971 by Canadian activists. It was known for taking bold and highly visible direct action, such as sailing, in 1972, into waters in the South Pacific to stop a nuclear test by the French government. The radical Earth First! was formed in 1980 as a response to what organizers felt was reticence on the part of more "mainstream" environmental groups.

At the political level, "Green" parties began to organize political activity at the national level. The first Green Party was formed in New Zealand in 1972, followed by one in Britain in 1973, Germany in 1979, and in the United States in 1996. Despite the publicity created around environmental issues with Green Party politics, electoral success was difficult in the face of established party politics. In Germany and New Zealand, the Greens achieved the most political power.

Political awareness and grassroots activity also spread to the Eastern Bloc during the last years of the Cold War. In Eastern Europe, in the late 1980s, environmental concerns were linked with issues of national autonomy. Environmentalists claimed that Soviet Communism, with its unrelenting focus on rapid modernization and industrialization, was responsible for a host of problems. These included water and air pollution, the damming of waterways for hydroelectricity, and nuclear power

John Muir (right), founder of the Sierra Club, with U.S. president Theodore Roosevelt, at Glacier Point in Yosemite National Park. Muir is considered to be one of the godfathers of the environmental movement.

plants that threatened long-term devastation, as happened at the Chernobyl reactor in 1986. Some historians claim that these environmental activists helped to bring an end to Soviet rule in 1991.

Grassroots activism could be found in the developing world as well. In Latin America, for instance, the passage of the Amazon Declaration in 1989 was due in part to a grassroots effort to preserve the region's rain forest and its biodiversity. In India, activists in the Chipko (meaning "embrace") movement put themselves between loggers and trees in efforts to reduce and stop deforestation. In 1993, protestors in Nigeria drew attention to the pollution caused by oil companies, helping to bring about **mitigation** programs. Some groups joined forces with Western groups, such as Greenpeace International, as globalization helped to make connections among activists worldwide.

The *Rainbow Warrior*, the flagship of the activist group Greenpeace, founded in 1971, at port in Genoa, Italy.

Text-Dependent Questions

1. Name and describe one environmental crisis that was important in triggering the public's awareness of environmental issues.

2. What was the Kyoto Protocol?

3. How does deforestation relate to climate change?

Research Projects

1. Research one of the environment disasters discussed in the chapter. Create a poster with images and captions explaining the event.

2. Select one environmental group mentioned in the chapter. Research its founding, the issues it addresses, and the kinds of tactics it uses to address its concerns.

Educational Videos

Chico Mendes and the Fight to Save the Amazon
Page 31
An excerpt from *A Fierce Green Fire* about Chico Mendez and the Brazilian rubber tappers he organized; includes actual footage of their protests against ranchers who were cutting down large tracts of the rain forest in the Amazon.

Published on YouTube by PBS *American Masters*.
https://www.youtube.com/watch?v=TdD42SBovfY.

The *Exxon Valdez* Disaster: 20 Years Later
Page 37
A short video showing the effects of the 1989 *Exxon Valdez* oil spill—both at the time and twenty years after it happened.

Published on YouTube by World Wildlife Fund.
https://youtu.be/MbjC9SMKClE.

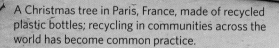

A Christmas tree in Paris, France, made of recycled plastic bottles; recycling in communities across the world has become common practice.

WORDS TO UNDERSTAND

carbon footprints: measures of the amount of impact a person has on greenhouse gas emissions.

fertility: expectations about how many children, on average, women will give birth to.

hydroelectric: relating to electricity produced by the force of running water.

incentives: actions, rules, or behaviors that spur a particular response.

malnutrition: inadequate nutrition due to a lack of food with the components required for healthy functioning and growth.

mortality: expectation about how long, on average, people will live.

CHAPTER
5

To The Present and Beyond

In the first two decades of the twenty-first century, changes that the environmental movement worked for filtered into the mainstream. Communities began to recycle, grade school classrooms discussed climate change, and laws and regulations were passed—from the UN Convention on the Law of the Sea to clean air and water legislation at the national level. Sustainability—making human activity, especially economic development, sensitive to the long-term health of people and the planet—had become the watchword.

Despite people coalescing around issues, however, changing international and domestic policies was not easy. Resistance from industry groups and private companies held strong, including ongoing pushback from energy companies. Sometimes companies aim to make the transition, but **incentives**—such as the tendency of American public to buy large cars and SUVs—point them in the opposite direction.

Even in the face of such challenges, the world is further along compared to the concerns and alarms of the 1960s and 1970s. As discussed below, there has been progress, but there is still a long way to go on many issues.

Population by the Numbers

Even though the predictions that Paul Ehrlich made in the 1960s about population growth were high, the numbers are still startling. As of 2015, 7.3 billion people called the Earth their home—nearly tripling the total from 1950 of 2.5 billion. That said, the growth rate has slowed in recent years. According to the UN's *Population Prospects: 2015 Revision* (UNPP2015), the year-to-year growth rate was 1.2 percent in 2005, and as of 2015, it dropped to 1.18 percent. While this might seem like a small drop, if it accumulates year over year, it will translate into a considerable slowing of population growth.

Indeed, the UN projects a continued decline in population growth in the future. But while the future growth rates may slow, the population is still growing. The world is projected to add 4 billion people by the end of the current century, according to the

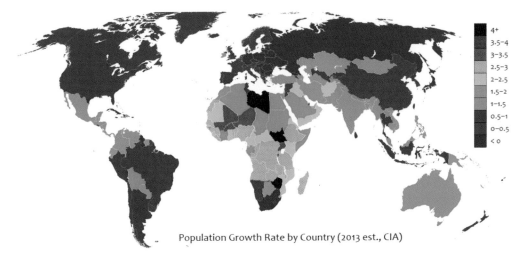

Population Growth Rate by Country (2013 est., CIA)

A chart created by the Central Intelligence Agency showing estimated 2013 population growth rates around the world; the highest rates are in Africa, with many nations experiencing 2.5 to 3 percent growth rates or higher.

UNPP2015. Its analysis shows an increase to 8.5 billion in 2030, to 9.5 billion in 2050, and to 11.2 billion in 2100. Stated another way, the number of people on the Earth will increase 53 percent by the end of the century, compared to 2015 levels.

In order to make these projections, assumptions were made about **fertility** and **mortality**. The UN, in making its predictions, determined that there would be a "decline of fertility for countries where large families are still prevalent," but a small increase in some countries where women have fewer than two children. The figures also assume that mortality will improve—more people will live longer—across the board, in all countries.

Most of the world's population growth in recent years has come from a group of forty-eight countries in the UN's "least developed countries" (LDCs) category. These include twenty-seven nations in Africa. Even though the growth rate of this group will slow, the total population of LDCs will likely double by 2050—reaching 1.9 billion in 2050, up from 954 million in 2015. By the end of the century, the population of this group will reach 3.2 billion. According to the UNPP2015, combining poverty and high growth rates spells problems: "The concentration of population growth in the poorest countries will make it harder for those governments to eradicate poverty and inequality, combat hunger and **malnutrition**, expand education enrollment and health systems, improve the provision of basic services, and implement other elements of a sustainable development agenda to ensure that no-one is left behind."

The news is not all grim. For instance, one of the reasons for the projected increase in Africa's growth rate is the improvement in life expectancy there in recent years. More children survive childbirth and early infancy due to improvements in health care. Because of that, an increasing number of people will reach adulthood and have children—resulting in a natural, yet sharp, increase in population. Improvements in health care affect life expectancy at the other end. People live longer and therefore contribute to expanding the population base.

Hunger and Food Security

Population numbers tell only one part of the story. What is the condition of people's lives? What about their ability to feed themselves and their families? Goal 1 of the UN's Millennium Development Goals (MDG), established in 2000, was to eradicate extreme poverty and hunger. And some progress was achieved by 2015, the end of the MDG monitoring period. One of the targets in this area—to halve the number of people living in extreme poverty—was reached by that year.

According to the FAO publication, *The State of Food Insecurity in the World, 2015*, the number of undernourished people globally dropped by 167 million from 2005 to a total of 795 million in 2015. Since 1990-1992, it had dropped by 216 million. And the drop is bigger in developing countries, even though they've experienced relatively higher population growth.

Oxfam, an NGO working on poverty issues across the world, has helped the famine-struck people of eastern Ethiopia; in 2011 the group trucked in clean water as poor rains dried up local sources.

Vast problems still exist, however. According to the FAO's 2015 report, more "progress has been hindered by slower and less inclusive economic growth as well as political instability in some developing regions." Access to fresh, clean drinking water is a growing problem in many parts of the developing world. Famine is widespread and recurs with frequency in parts of Asia and Africa. In the African nation of Ethiopia, for instance, a severe famine that began in 2015 has been aggravated by an extreme El Niño weather pattern. Whether extreme El Niño events are related to global climate change—a claim made more and more by climate scientists—the fluctuations in temperature and precipitation resulting from them are certainly real. In eastern Ethiopia, large groups of people are experiencing "significant food consumption gaps," according to USAID's Fact Sheet on the country. The northeast and central parts of the country are experiencing the worst drought in over fifty years.

This is nothing new in the region. In 1985 and 1986, the biggest drought in a century struck an area that is now part of Ethiopia and Eritrea. Some 8 million people were affected by the resulting famine, and estimates run as high as 1 million dead, according to "Hunger and Food Security" in *World at Risk: A Global Issues Sourcebook*. Record low rainfalls were aggravated by economic demands on the agricultural sector by the government, including a "famine relief tax" in some parts of the country. Growing increasingly authoritative, the government was also fighting an insurgency and devoted more and more of its economic output to the military—upwards of 46 percent by 1984.

These kinds of factors—government mismanagement, civil war, recurring weather events, chronic rainfall shortages—translate into a vicious cycle for many regions already experiencing food shortages. And outside aid has a way of being unreliable. Humanitarian aid kicked in during the 1980s crisis, but what some people call "donor fatigue" factored into the 2015–2016 famine. Many emergencies took a back seat to the deepening and widening crises in war-torn Syria and Iraq and the resulting refugee crisis.

THE SAHEL

Not just in Ethiopia, but across the northern part of Africa in the Sahel region, drought is endemic and frequent. Since the 1970s, the Sahel has undergone severe desertification. Its semiarid climate, which supports a nomadic lifestyle—involving cattle grazing as the rainfall shifts throughout the year—has been slowly becoming drier.

Despite international efforts, such as the 1994 UN Convention to Combat Desertification, the region remains vulnerable to drought. A third harsh drought in a decade hit the region in 2012, affecting more than 18 million people. It came on the heels of serious food crises in 2008 and 2010. Some accounts show increased rainfall in the Sahel over the last decade, but the region will continue to be famine prone and food insecure until long-term environmental and economic solutions are developed.

Climate Change

Droughts in developed countries may also be linked to climate change, according to many researchers. An extended dry period in the western part of the United States called attention to this possibility. The state of California, in fact, imposed water restriction measures for the first time in its history in April 2015. According to the U.S. Drought Monitor, run by the University of Nebraska–Lincoln, only a small sliver of land in the extreme northwest of the state, along the coast, is free from drought. And close to two-thirds of the state is under "extreme" or "exceptional" drought conditions.

Much of the region relies on snowpack in the Sierras Mountains to supply water for the land to the west of the range. Snowpack releases water more slowly, allowing it to absorb into the surrounding watershed more readily. But with more rain and less snow falling in the Sierras, California's drought conditions now seem more endemic than occasional.

Climate change, though, is a global phenomenon. Greenhouse gases are trapped in the atmosphere, which circulates around the Earth. They travel relatively freely, above the Earth, no matter what company or country emits them. And the increased accumulation of greenhouse gasses in the atmosphere is clear and undeniable. Emissions of carbon dioxide have risen by some 90 percent, from 1970 to the early 2010s, according the U.S. Environmental Protection Agency (EPA).The main

In January 2014, the mountains of Lassen Volcanic National Park, in northeast California, showed no signs of the usual winter snowpack; a serious drought has caused water shortages throughout much of the state since that time.

DEFORESTATION AND BIODIVERSITY

According to the FAO, the world loses some 18 million acres (7.4 million hectares) of forests every year. Forests in Afghanistan have been reduced by over 70 percent since the late 1990s. Since the 1960s, the Amazon rain forests have lost 17 percent, mostly to cattle grazing, but also due to harvesting mahogany, gold, and oil, according to World Wide Fund for Nature. Tropical rain forests, such as in the Amazon region, are particularly valuable due to their biodiversity. Rain forests in the tropics are home to some 80 percent of the world's species, and loss of even small tracts can endanger species. In addition to the loss of biodiversity, losing tracts of trees often increases soil erosion, as trees and their root systems hold soil in place. Fewer trees to absorb carbon dioxide also increases greenhouse gasses in the atmosphere.

contributors to emissions—around 78 percent—are engines running fossil fuels and industrial processes, according to the EPA. The next highest impact comes from agriculture, deforestation, and other changes in land use.

An especially thorny issue is the changing fortunes of rising developing countries, such as India and China. As these countries develop their economies and provide for their populations, their "**carbon footprints**" undoubtedly increase. Everything that comes with increased wealth—from the increased need for power to widespread car ownership—increases greenhouse gas emissions.

Smog in Beijing, China, is a common occurrence, as seen in this photo from December 2015.

This all contributes, many believe, to general warming trends. According to the UN, the year 2015 was the hottest year on record. It was also the culmination of a long-term warming trend: the five-year period ending in 2015, according to World Resources Institute (WRI) Web page, Climate Milestones of 2015, was the warmest on record, and the last three decades were each warmer than any other ten-year period recorded. The WRI further states that the last time recorded annual global temperature was below average was in 1975. According to the EPA, as of 2011 the biggest emitters of CO_2 were China, at 28 percent, and the United States, at 16 percent.

Addressing Climate Change

The goals for current climate policy have been hard to reach, given the complex needs and interests of those involved in the debate. It has even been difficult to reach a consensus on the facts surrounding climate change. In the IPCC's third report, from 2001, however, its conclusions became more specific and quantitative. And more national science academies—including those from Brazil, Canada, China, India, France, Germany, and India—joined the IPCC in concluding with 90 percent certainty that "temperatures will continue to rise, with average global surface temperature projected to increase by between 1.4 and 5.8 degrees C [2.5 to 10.4 degrees F] above 1990 levels by 2100." The "Summary for Policymakers" from its 2013 assessment stated that "warming of the climate system is unequivocal, and since the 1950s, many of the observed changes are unprecedented over decades to millennia."

An international exhibition outside the negotiation center at the COP21 climate talks in Paris, December 2015.

As the science was being nailed down, world leaders and policy makers have had an equally hard time forging a common path. That said, in December 2015, a world agreement was hammered out at the climate talks in Paris—referred to as COP21. A target—of holding the increase in global warming to 2.7 to 3.6 degrees F (1.5 to 2 degrees C)—was established. With China and the United States, the largest emitters, on board, the agreement holds some promise of success.

A compromise—long in coming—was also reached on assistance to developing nations for curtailing their emissions and developing alternative energies. Working out a trade-off had been a sticking point. Developing nations had long claimed that they shouldn't be asked to share the burden of reducing emissions equally, when industrialized wealthier nations created the problems in the first place. The specifics of a solution were finally agreed upon in Paris. They evolved around wealthier countries increasing their support for less-developed nations in their transition to renewable energy, in exchange for them agreeing to lower emissions.

Whether this all will work out is a big question. There are many ways the agreement could fall apart. The internal politics of the United States is critical: it must stick to the agreement, even as the Congress, president, and administrations change. The political and economic landscape in China is also critical. Will the ruling Communist Party of China—likely to last for a long time—feel the need to adjust its stance if economic growth, already a nagging issue, continues to be threatened? Also, the nature of the agreement itself may give rise to problems. The COP21 agreement outlines targets and strategies but leaves some specifics to a later date. As has happened in the past, nailing down the details may stall the process.

Pollution

The understanding of how pollutants work in the environment has grown dramatically since Rachel Carson first described DDT as poisonous to birds and other wildlife. In 2001 the Stockholm Convention on Persistent Organic Pollutants was passed as an international mechanism to monitor chemicals and analyze their environmental effects. Many individual countries had banned many such chemicals, but the United Nations Environment Programme pushed the convention as a way to bring global attention to the harmful effects of persistent organic pollutants (POPs).

The convention originally listed twelve chemicals—the "dirty dozen" as some refer to them. These include such pesticides as DDT and endrin, used against insects and rodents. Other well-known POPs on the original list include polychlorinated biphenyls, or PCBs, which are used as additives in paints and plastics; and dioxins, which are produced as by-products of the high-temperature burning of municipal waste, for instance, and emissions from cars. Added to the list since 2001 were more pesticides as well as other chemicals used in building and industrial processes, including a flame retardant, HBCD, that is used in insulation and interior upholstery for cars.

Classifying such chemicals as POPs draws attention to the fact that they do not break down easily in the environment. Samples of HBCD, for instance, have shown up in birds, mammals, fish, and soil. In addition, POPs "bioaccumulate," meaning they increase in organisms higher up on the food chain. This means that, in humans, they exist in concentrations higher than they would in the environment.

Air pollution and water pollution have also been at the top of the agenda, especially for newly industrializing countries. Measures to address those problems are also advancing. India, for instance, adopted vehicle emissions standards similar to those in Europe in 2005. That said, cars and trucks predating those standards are still on the roads. China, for its part, has faced massive air quality problems as well: according to the 2007 report of the country's State Environmental Protection Administration, thirty-nine cities faced severe air pollution conditions. Its measures to address these issues struggle to keep up with the problems arising from rapid economic growth.

Traffic congestion at an intersection in Kolkata, India; as the country modernizes, the number of cars on the road increases dramatically.

China's rivers are also at risk. The Yangtze (Chang) River, one of world's longest and one of China's most important waterways, is also one of the world's most polluted. While its river basin is home to one-third of the Chinese people, it is fouled—in many sections—by industrial discharge and agricultural runoff. In 2008 a tributary, called the Han, ran "red and foamy," according to the *International Herald Tribune*, likely due to high levels of ammonia, nitrogen, and permanganate, a chemical used in cleaning and bleaching processes. In 2012, a section of the Yangtze around Chongqing, in central China, also turned red, and the same happened in 2014 on the Wenzhou River in eastern China.

A protestor outside Japan's embassy in London, in 2012, taking a stand against nuclear power after an earthquake and tsunami hit Japan, causing a meltdown at the Fukushima Daiichi nuclear power plant.

The Nuclear Question and Alternative Energy

Advocates of nuclear power were forced to reconsider its safety in March 11, 2011, when a "triple disaster" hit the east coast of Japan. After a massive earthquake—measuring 9.0 on the Richter scale—hit off of the country's coast, a huge tsunami, rising 49 feet (15 meters), swept inland and flooded the reactors at the Fukushima Daiichi nuclear power plant. Meltdowns occurred in three reactors, as coolant was lost due to the damage from the tsunami. Fifteen days after the event, radioactivity in trace amounts was detected across the entire Northern Hemisphere. It was the largest nuclear disaster since Chernobyl.

No people died from immediate exposure to the radiation that leaked during the meltdowns—though close to 16,000 people died as a result of the tsunami and earthquake. The long-term health effects, however, are uncertain and still to be revealed. For instance, the risk of developing thyroid cancer for female infants in the immediate vicinity has been estimated to be 70 percent above normal.

The disaster traumatized Japan and shocked the world. Japan began reevaluating its nuclear energy policy almost immediately after the disaster occurred. France did the same, and soon after it announced that it would scale back its nuclear power capacity by a third. Germany announced that it would accelerate already existing plans to phase out its reactors by 2022.

Other countries, such as Malaysia and the Philippines, decided to stay the course. China, which initially put its nuclear expansion programs on hold, restarted them quickly and was on track to triple its output from nuclear power by 2020. Russia and India are also pressing ahead, as is Britain, despite public protests. In the United States, which had not built a new nuclear power plant in thirty years, the high cost of building new facilities had curbed the enthusiasm for developing new ones by 2011, and the triple disaster in Japan gave further pause for investing in them.

Given these potential setbacks in nuclear power, renewable energy sources have become more important. As China attempts to deal with extreme pollution problems from coal-based energy, it has invested heavily in renewables. As of 2014 it leads the world in terms of electricity generated from alternative sources, according to the U.S. Energy Information Administration (EIA). It has done this in part through **hydroelectric** power, which itself creates controversy due to the construction of dams in many parts of the country.

Significantly, the world market for petroleum has suffered, with a plunge in oil prices starting in the middle of 2014 to record low levels in 2016. Whether this downturn will be the new normal is the subject of great debate. And whether it will affect investment in developing alternative forms of energy is an open question.

A Long Way from Crop Dusting

Crop dusting, the agricultural innovation that took off so much after World War II, has been replaced by other interventions in the environment. Genetic engineering and the development of genetically modified organisms (GMOs) has begun to supplant the need for chemical fertilizers and pesticides.

Seeking insect resistance in food crops through the use of DDT and other pesticides and higher yields to feed growing populations in the developing world through the Green Revolution began this story. The concerns raised by Rachel Carson and other early warners set the world on a crusade to take care of the planet. Learning the best ways to be stewards of the planet has been, and continues to be, a long-term project. But it is critical that we learn these lessons—for the protection of our food supply, for the health of the human population, and for the long-term sustainability of economic and social development.

A protest against GMOs in Chile in August 2013.

Text-Dependent Questions

1. What does the United Nations project the world population to be in the years 2050 and 2100?

2. Describe the cycle that caused famine in Ethiopia in the late 1960s and early 1970s.

3. What are persistent organic pollutants (POPs)?

Research Projects

1. Select an environmental issue covered in this chapter and write a report exploring the current status and the future predictions concerning the issue. Use the data and sources mentioned in the chapter as starting points.

2. Divide into groups to debate whether nuclear power should be banned or continued. Use information in the chapter, but also expand your knowledge and arguments with data and other material from your library or the Internet.

Timeline

1946	A baby boom begins in most nations involved in World War II.
1950	Chemical factories in the United States are producing 2.6 million tons/year of a fertilizer called anhydrous ammonia.
	The planet is home to 2.5 billion people; India and China are the two most populous countries, as they still are in 2016.
1952	High levels of smog hit London, causing the immediate death of some 4,000 people; thousands more die in the following weeks.
	The disastrous effects of water pollution are seen when the Cuyahoga River in Ohio, in the United States, catches fire.
1954	The Office of Food for Peace is established under U.S. president Dwight D. Eisenhower.
1956	The International Atomic Energy Agency is created, becoming the main international organization charged with controlling the spread of nuclear weapons.
	Britain passes the Clean Air Act, one of the earliest attempts in the modern era to reduce the effects of air pollution.
mid-1960s	Dr. Norman Borlaug's Green Revolution—focused on increasing rice and wheat crop yields—helps to address famine in India.
1961	American scientist Charles Keeling charts yearly increases in atmospheric CO_2 levels, having begun monitoring them at the Mauna Loa Observatory in Hawaii in 1958.
	USAID begins under U.S. president John F. Kennedy; food aid becomes more responsive to countries in need, separate from the interests of American farmers.
	Rachel Carson's *Silent Spring* is published; in it, she warns about the long-term effects of chemicals, including pesticides, on the environment and on human health.
	The World Wildlife Fund (now World Wide Fund for Nature) is established.
1962	France's nuclear energy program begins, when its first nuclear power plant comes on line.
1963	The UN establishes the World Food Programme to offer direct food assistance to countries in times of stress and crisis.
1968	Paul Ehrlich's *The Population Bomb* is published, sounding an alarm about the pressure that population growth was putting on the world's resources.
1970	Activists organize the first Earth Day; the National Environmental Policy Act establishes the U.S. Environmental Protection Agency, and the Clean Air Act is also passed.

1971	Greenpeace is established by Canadian activists.
1972	The Clean Water Act is passed in the United States; it is revised in 1977 and again, with the Water Quality Act, in 1987.
	The UN Conference on the Human Environment is held in Stockholm; it results in the establishment of the UN Environment Programme that year.
1974	Australia establishes the Australian Development Assistance Agency (now under AusAID) to help countries reduce poverty.
1976	Sixteen nations adopt the Mediterranean Action Plan to address concerns with pollution in their regional waters.
1982	The UN Convention on the Law of the Sea (UNCLOS) is adopted.
1985	British researchers discover an "ozone hole" in the Earth's atmosphere above Antarctica.
1985–1986	The biggest drought in a century strikes the area now part of Ethiopia and Eritrea; some 8 million people are affected by the resulting famine.
1986	The most serious nuclear accident of all time occurs in the Ukraine, then part of the Soviet Union, at the Chernobyl Nuclear Power Plant.
1989	Countries in South America sign the Amazon Declaration, which advocates for the preservation of "our Amazon heritage."
1992	The Rio Earth Summit takes place; it aims to translate Agenda 21 into action, including the UN Framework Convention on Climate Change.
1994	The first GMO food—a slow-ripening tomato—hits U.S. grocery shelves; by 1997, the European Union requires foods made with GMO ingredients to be labeled.
1996	The Kyoto Protocol is signed, but later weakened in 2001, when U.S. president George W. Bush withdraws the United States from the agreement.
2001	The Stockholm Convention on Persistent Organic Pollutants is passed to monitor chemicals and analyze their environmental effects.
2006	The World Health Organization recommends the use of DDT, despite a worldwide agricultural ban, to fight malaria in highly affected countries.
2010	An explosion on BP Petroleum's *Deepwater Horizon* kills eleven crew members and causes a huge oil spill in the Gulf of Mexico.
2010s	Global emissions of carbon dioxide rise by some 90 percent from 1970; GMOs dominate food production across the globe.
2015	According to the UN, this year is the hottest on record, while 7.3 billion people call the Earth their home—nearly tripling the total of 2.5 billion from 1950.
	A world agreement is reached at climate talks in Paris, with a target of holding the increase in global warming to 2.7 to 3.6 degrees F (1.5 to 2 degrees C).

Further Research

BOOKS

Bedford, Daniel, and John Cook. *Climate Change: Examining the Facts*. Santa Barbara, CA: ABC-CLIO, 2016.

Lytle, Mark Hamilton. *The Gentle Subversive: Rachel Carson, Silent Spring, and the Rise of the Modern Environmental Movement*. New York: Oxford University Press, 2007.

Miller, Char, ed. *The Atlas of U.S. and Canadian Environmental History*. New York: Routledge, 2003.

Newton, David E. *The Global Water Crisis: A Reference Handbook*. Santa Barbara, CA: ABC-CLIO, 2016.

Tabak, John. *Energy and the Environment*. 6 vols. New York: Facts On File, 2009.

World at Risk: A Global Issues Sourcebook. 2nd ed. Washington, DC: CQ Press, 2010.

ONLINE

Food and Agriculture Organization of the United Nations: http://www.fao.org/home/en/.

Population Reference Bureau: http://www.prb.org/.

United Nations Environment Programme: http://www.unep.org.

United Nations Sustainable Development Goals: http://www.undp.org/content/undp/en/home/sdgoverview/

World Watch Institute: http://www.worldwatch.org/.

NOTE TO EDUCATORS: This book contains both imperial and metric measurements as well as references to global practices and trends in an effort to encourage the student to gain a worldly perspective. We, as publishers, feel it's our role to give young adults the tools they need to thrive in a global society.

Index

Italicized page numbers refer to illustrations

Index (continued)

Photo Credits

Page number	Page location	Archive/Photographer
8	Top	Shutterstock/ermess
10	Top	National Archives and Records Administration/ Tennessee Valley Authority
11	Bottom	Wikimedia Commons/National Archives and Records Administration
12	Top	Wikimedia Commons/OSU Special Collections & Archives
12	Bottom	Wikimedia Commons/kallerna
14	Top	Shutterstock/Robin Nieuwenkamp
16	Bottom	Wikimedia Commons/National Archives and Records Administration, Russell Lee
17	Top	Wikimedia Commons/National Archives and Records Administration
18	Bottom	International Maize and Wheat Improvement Center (CIMMYT) photo archives, www.cimmyt.org
19	Bottom	Wikimedia Commons/U.S. Fish and Wildlife Service, Rex Gary Schmidt
20	Bottom	Wikimedia Commons/U.S. Navy
22	Top	Shutterstock/Shanti Hesse
24	Top	Wikimedia Commons/Paul R. Ehrlich
25	Bottom	Wikimedia Commons/Pacomartin
26	Bottom	Wikimedia Commons/U.S. Postal Service; Bureau of Engraving and Printing, Stevan Dohanos
27	Top	Wikimedia Commons/USAID U.S. Agency for International Development
28	Bottom	Wikimedia Commons/CDC, Dr. Lyle Conrad
30	Top	iStock/luoman
32	Top	Wikimedia Commons/Miranda Smith
33	Bottom	Cleveland Memory Project, Cleveland State University, Michael Schwartz Library, Special Collections, Joseph E. Cole
34	Bottom	Shutterstock/Signature Message
35	Bottom	Wikimedia Commons/National Archives and Records Administration, Environmental Protection Agency, David Falconer
36	Bottom	Wikimedia Commons/Elena Filatova
37	Bottom	Wikimedia Commons/Delorme
39	Bottom	iStock/Bernhard_Staehli
41	Bottom	Library of Congress/Underwood & Underwood
42	Bottom	Wikimedia Commons/Davide from Bologna
44	Top	Shutterstock/Artesia Wells
46	Top	Wikimedia Commons/Kwamikagami
47	Bottom	Wikimedia Commons/Oxfam East Africa
49	Bottom	Wikimedia Commons/LassenNPS
50	Bottom	Shutterstock/testing
51	Bottom	Wikimedia Commons/Surfnico
53	Bottom	Wikimedia Commons/Biswarup Ganguly
54	Bottom	Shutterstock/Stuart Monk
56	Bottom	Wikimedia Commons/Mapuexpress Informativo Mapuche
Cover	Top	Shutterstock/Everett Historical
Cover	Left	Shutterstock/Alzbeta
Cover	Right	Shutterstock/FloridaStock

About the Author and Advisor

Series Advisor

Ruud van Dijk teaches the history of international relations at the University of Amsterdam, the Netherlands. He studied history at Amsterdam, the University of Kansas, and Ohio University, where he obtained his Ph.D. in 1999. He has also taught at Carnegie Mellon University, Dickinson College, and the University of Wisconsin-Milwaukee, where he also served as editor at the Center for 21st Century Studies. He has published on the East-West conflict over Germany during the Cold War, the controversies over nuclear weapons in the 1970s and 1980s, and the history of globalization. He is the senior editor of the *Encyclopedia of the Cold War* (2008), produced with MTM Publishing and published by Routledge.

Author

Valerie Tomaselli is an editor and writer, who has worked on a wide range of books in such fields as global studies, history, and arts and culture. She is the founder and president of MTM Publishing, an award-winning editorial-services and book-producing company, where she has led the team responsible for a long list of acclaimed books for such clients as CQ Press, Charlesbridge, DK Publishing, Macmillan Reference, Mason Crest, Oxford University Press, Princeton University Press, Routledge, Sage, and the Sculpture Foundation. She currently serves as the series editor for *Foundations in Global Studies* for Routledge/Taylor & Francis.